D1558280

10/05

# They Are the Best!

## Mary Elizabeth Salzmann

Consulting Editor Monica Marx, M.A./Reading Specialist

Publishing Company

Published by SandCastle™, an imprint of ABDO Publishing Company, 4940 Viking Drive, Edina, Minnesota 55435.

Printed in the United States.

Credits
Edited by: Pam Price
Curriculum Coordinator: Nancy Tuminelly
Cover and Interior Design and Production: Mighty Media
Photo Credits: Brand X Pictures, Comstock, Corbis Images, PhotoDisc, Stockbyte

Library of Congress Cataloging-in-Publication Data

Salzmann, Mary Elizabeth, 1968-
    They are the best! / Mary Elizabeth Salzmann.
        p. cm. -- (Sight words)
    Includes index.
    Summary: Uses simple sentences, photographs, and a brief story to introduce six different words: a, do, has, the, their, they.
    ISBN 1-59197-474-7
    1. Readers (Primary) 2. Vocabulary--Juvenile literature. [1. Reading.] I. Title. II. Series.

PE1119.S234249 2003
428.1--dc21
                                                                    2003050326

SandCastle™ books are created by a professional team of educators, reading specialists, and content developers around five essential components that include phonemic awareness, phonics, vocabulary, text comprehension, and fluency. All books are written, reviewed, and leveled for guided reading, early intervention reading, and Accelerated Reader® programs and designed for use in shared, guided, and independent reading and writing activities to support a balanced approach to literacy instruction.

## Let Us Know

After reading the book, SandCastle would like you to tell us your stories about reading. What is your favorite page? Was there something hard that you needed help with? Share the ups and downs of learning to read. We want to hear from you! To get posted on the ABDO Publishing Company Web site, send us e-mail at:

**sandcastle@abdopub.com**

**SandCastle Level: Beginning**

# Featured Sight Words

a            do

has          the

their        they

Carl and his dad
make a birdhouse.

Nancy helps her
mom do the laundry.

Dave has fun with his dad.

**the**

Tess and her mom work in the garden.

Liz helps her dad
make their dinner.

They hold Rick
up high.

# Mei's Parents

Mei has a mom and a dad.

She likes to do things with her parents.

Mei and her mom
play the piano.

Mei and her dad
use their computer.

Mei thinks they are
the best parents!

# More Sight Words in This Book

| | |
|---|---|
| and | she |
| are | to |
| her | up |
| his | with |
| in | work |
| make | |

All words identified as sight words in this book are from Edward Bernard Fry's "First Hundred Instant Sight Words."

# Picture Index

**birdhouse,** p. 5

**computer,** p. 20

**dinner,** p. 13

**garden,** p. 11

**laundry,** p. 7

**piano,** p. 18

# About SandCastle™

A professional team of educators, reading specialists, and content developers created the SandCastle™ series to support young readers as they develop reading skills and strategies and increase their general knowledge. The SandCastle™ series has four levels that correspond to early literacy development in young children. The levels are provided to help teachers and parents select the appropriate books for young readers.

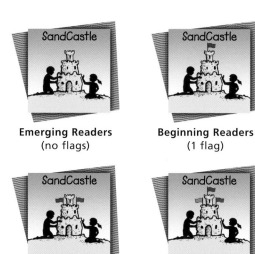

**Emerging Readers**
(no flags)

**Beginning Readers**
(1 flag)

**Transitional Readers**
(2 flags)

**Fluent Readers**
(3 flags)

These levels are meant only as a guide. All levels are subject to change.

To see a complete list of SandCastle™ books and other nonfiction titles from ABDO Publishing Company, visit **www.abdopub.com** or contact us at:

4940 Viking Drive, Edina, Minnesota 55435 • 1-800-800-1312 • fax: 1-952-831-1632